Amazing Rooftops

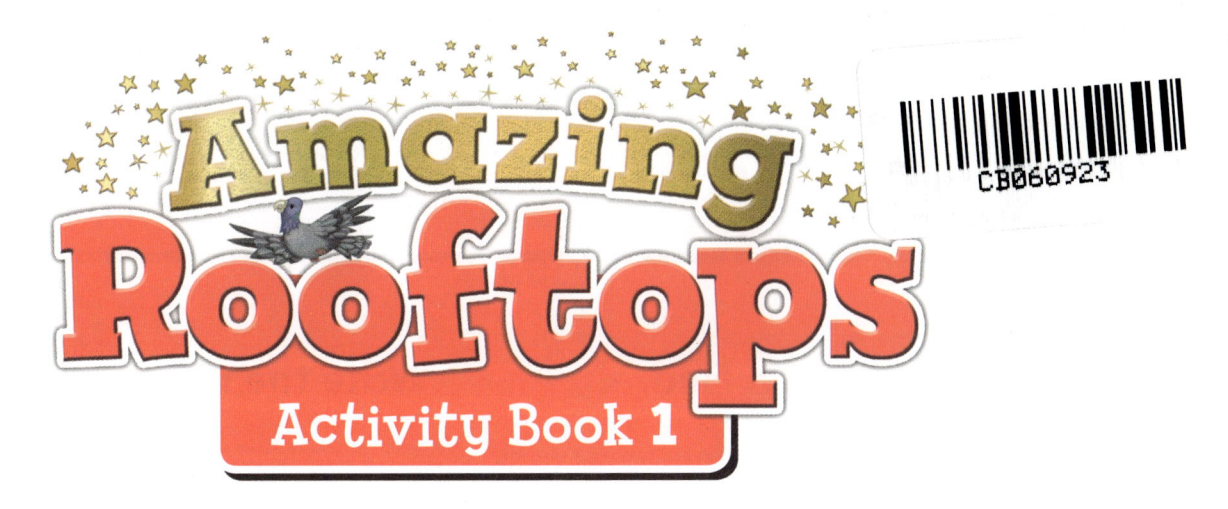

Activity Book 1

Helen Casey • Cheryl Palin • Julie Penn

Contents

Unit		Page
S	Welcome to Park Street	2
1	In the park	6
2	By the river	15
R	Rooftops Review 1	24
3	In the city	26
4	At the party	35
R	Rooftops Review 2	44
5	At the carnival	46
6	At the picnic	55
R	Rooftops Review 3	64
	Halloween	66
	Christmas	67
	Easter	68
	Culture mini-books	69

OXFORD UNIVERSITY PRESS

Lesson 1 Vocabulary

Starter: Welcome to Park Street

1 Trace and write. Find.   **2** Write the number.

1 2 3 4 5
6 7 10
8 9

I'm Nizzy. I'm ____.

I'm Anna. I'm 6.

I'm Oscar. I'm ____.

Lesson 2 Vocabulary

1 Trace. Look and colour.

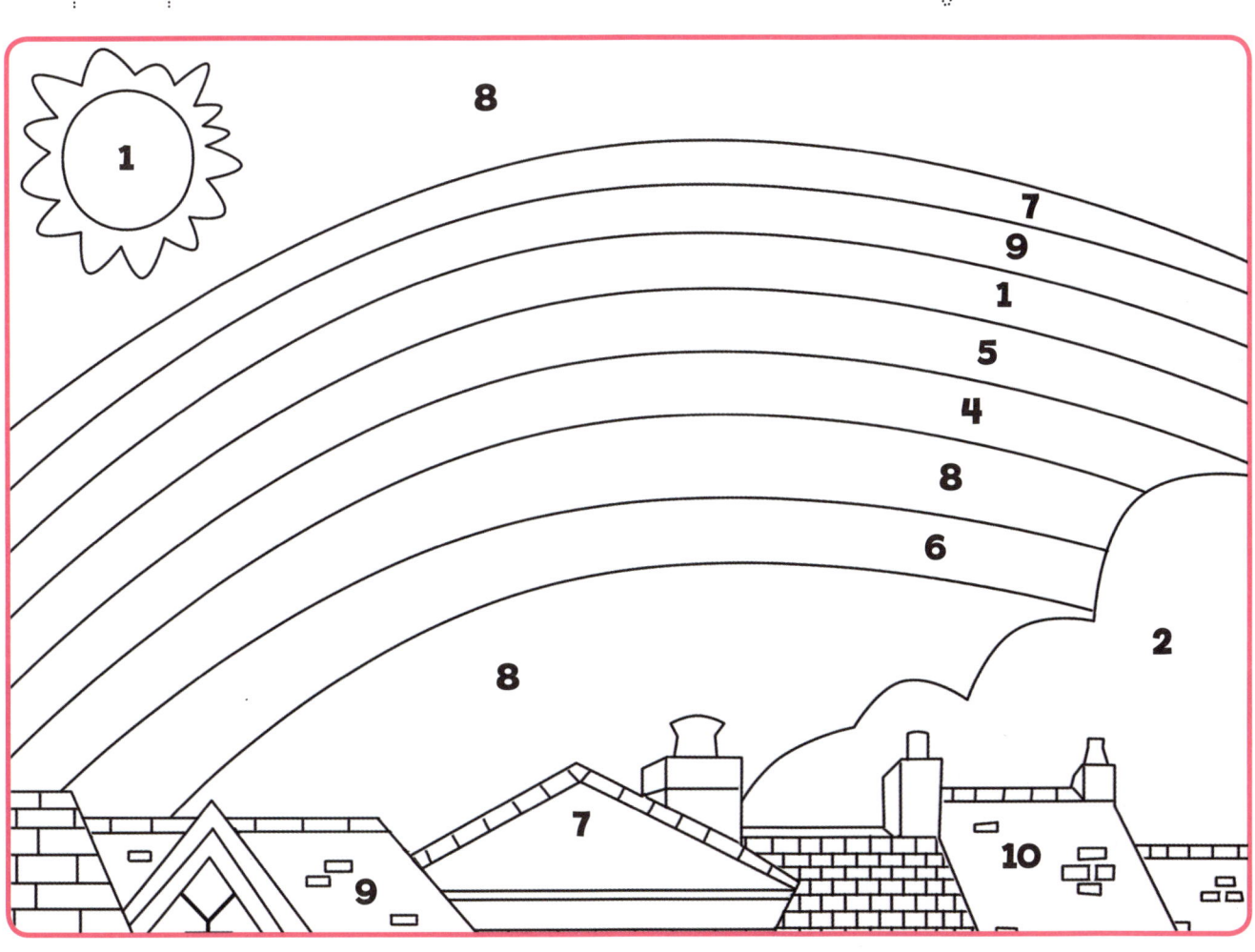

1. yellow
2. white
3. black
4. green
5. pink
6. purple
7. red
8. blue
9. orange
10. brown

Lesson 3 Vocabulary

1 Colour and find. Circle.

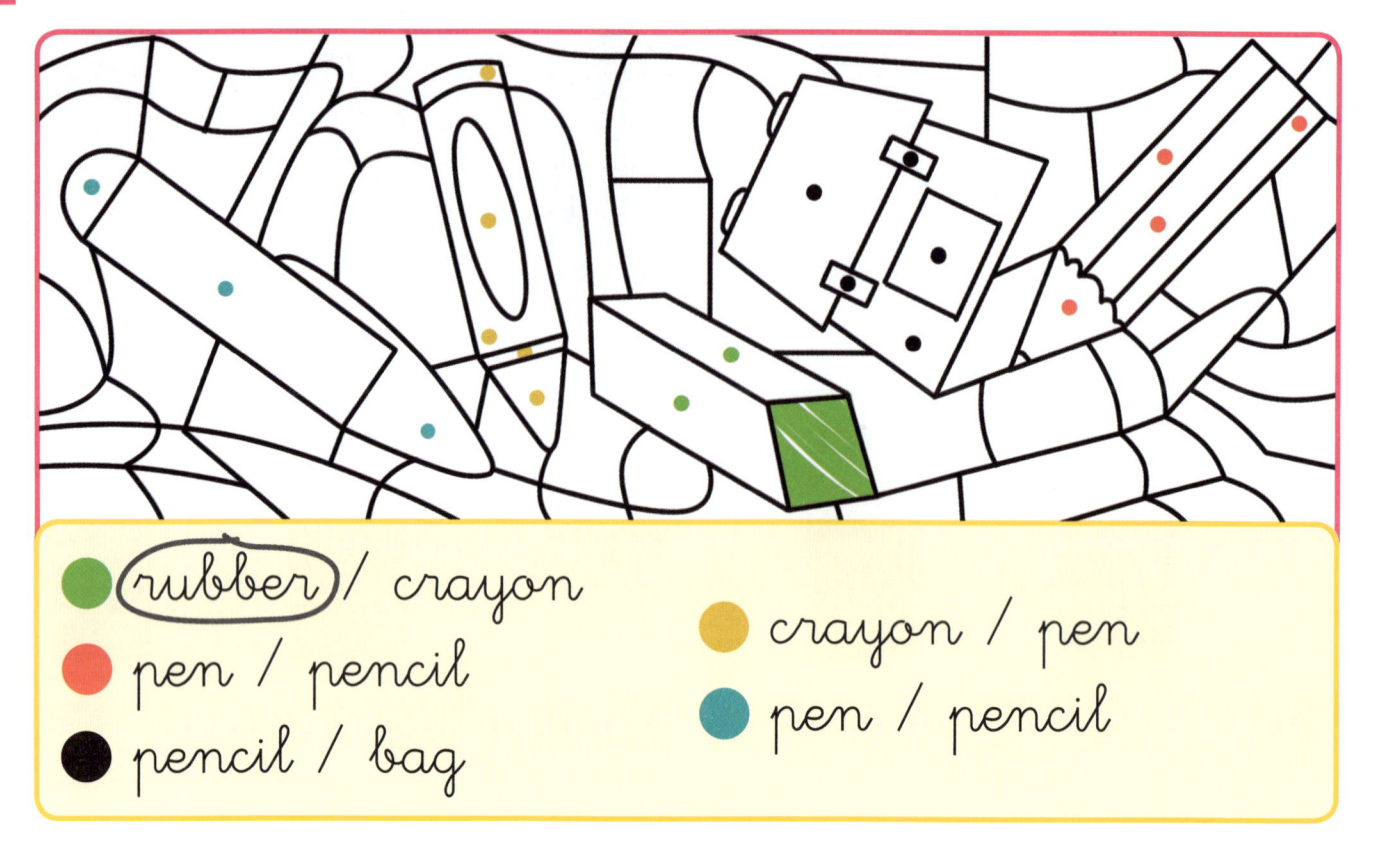

- 🟢 (rubber) / crayon
- 🟠 pen / pencil
- ⚫ pencil / bag
- 🟡 crayon / pen
- 🔵 pen / pencil

2 Match and trace.

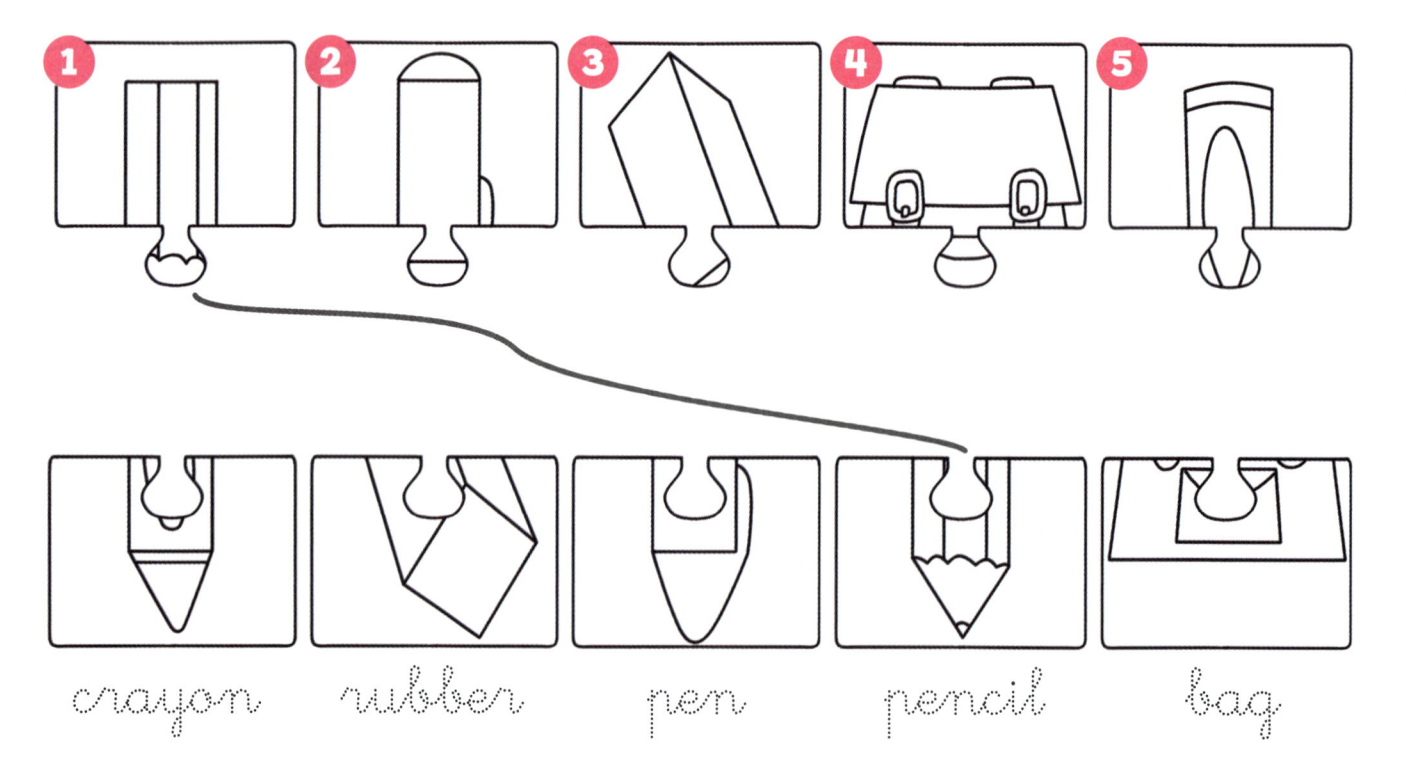

crayon   rubber   pen   pencil   bag

Lesson 4 Vocabulary and Literacy

1 🗨 Think Find and colour. Trace, count and write.

pen   5

pencil ☐

rubber ☐

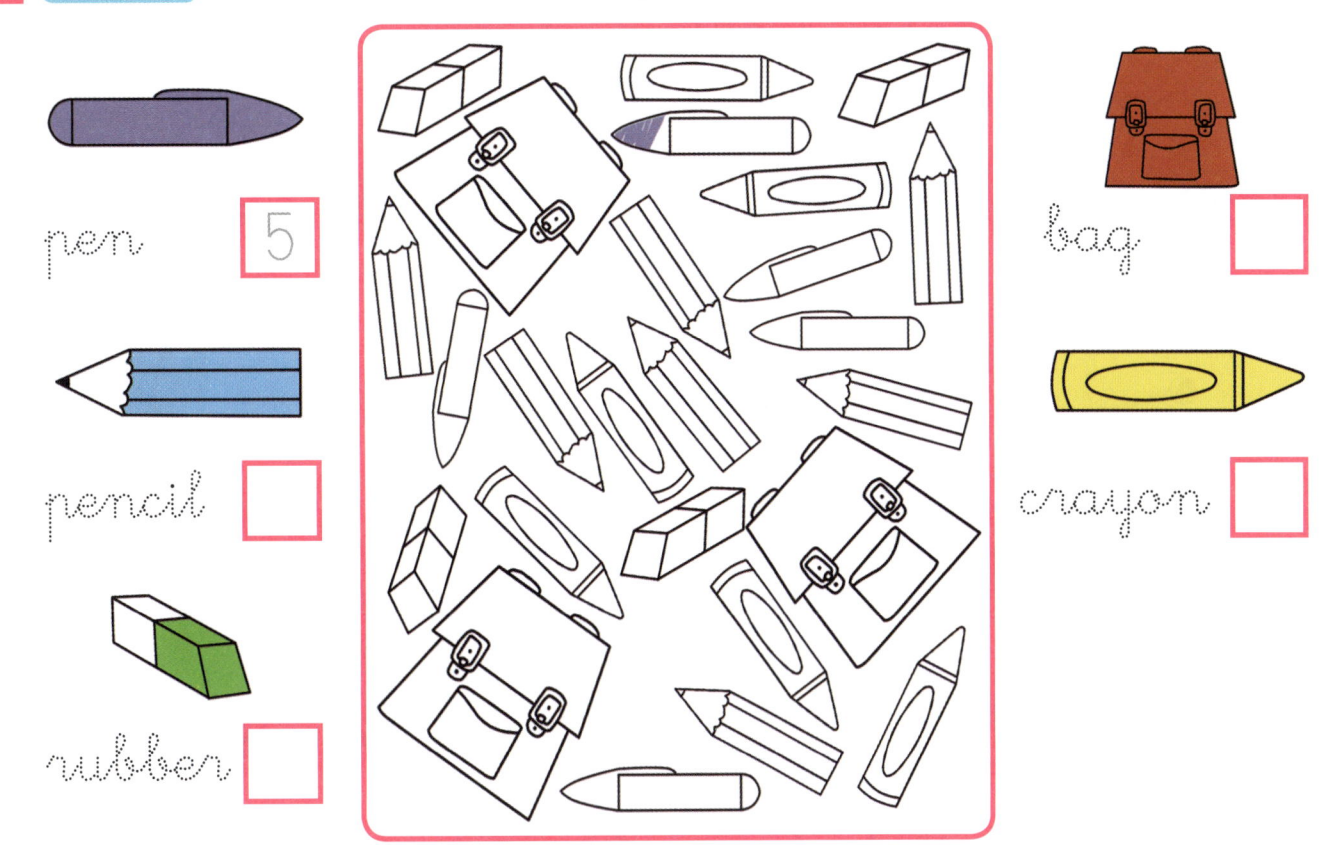

bag ☐

crayon ☐

Rooftops Book Club

2 Look and tick ✓ your reader. What's the title? Trace and match.

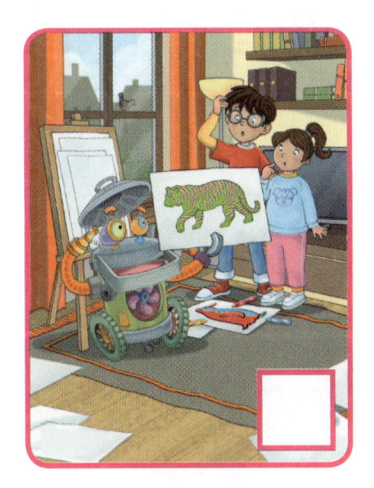

Hello, Clunk.   Hello!   I'm Clunk.

Book Club Extra
Write your name on your finger puppets.

Lesson 1 Vocabulary

1 In the park

1 Match and colour the toys. **2** Circle the toys you've got at home.

1. scooter
2. bike
3. doll
4. ball
5. skateboard
6. skipping rope
7. book
8. kite

Finished?
Draw the red toy and the green toy.

Lesson 2 Grammar **1**

1 Trace and tick ✓.

1.
scooter ✓
skipping rope ☐

2.
skateboard ☐
bike ☐

3.
book ☐
doll ☐

4.
kite ☐
ball ☐

2 Trace. Draw the missing toys.

I've got a scooter.

I've got a skipping rope.

Finished?
Write *I've got a* … Draw your toy.

7

Lesson 3 Culture

1 Listen, guess and number. 🔊 16

2 💡 Be creative — Draw you and your friends at playtime. Trace.

I've got a toy!

Lesson 4 Everyday language and Values 1

Our Values
Do you share?

1 💬 Think Look and colour the children sharing.
Look and tick ✔ the words in the picture.

pen ☐ pencil ✔ rubber ☐ ball ☐ book ☐ bag ☐

2 💬 Communicate What can you share? Trace. Act out at home.

This ball is for you.

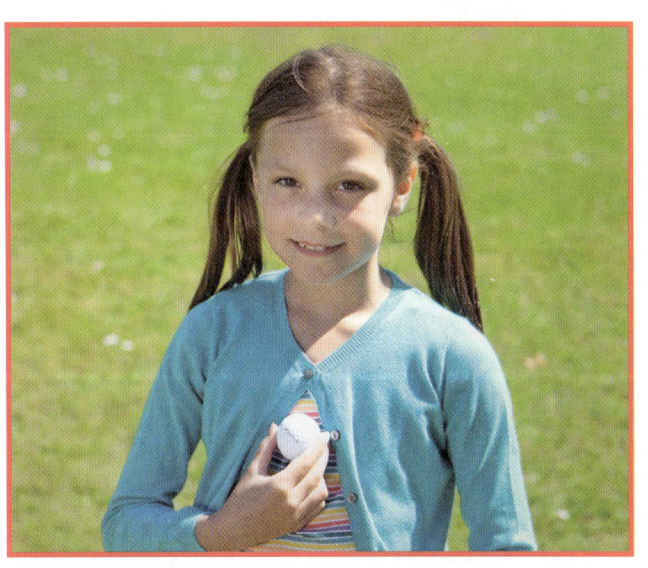

This ball is for me.

9

Lesson 5 Story

The park story

1 🗨 **Think** Match. Colour the hats.

I've got a hat.

2 💡 **Be creative** Draw yourself in your favourite hat from the story. Trace.

My favourite hat.

Finished?
Draw a hat for your friend. Write *This hat is for you.*

Lesson 6 Vocabulary and Grammar

1 Look and colour.

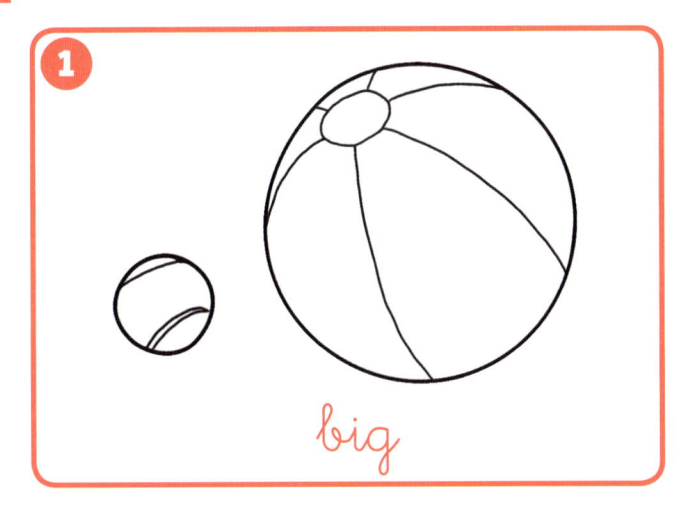

1. big
2. small
3. old
4. new

2 Draw and trace. Look and number.

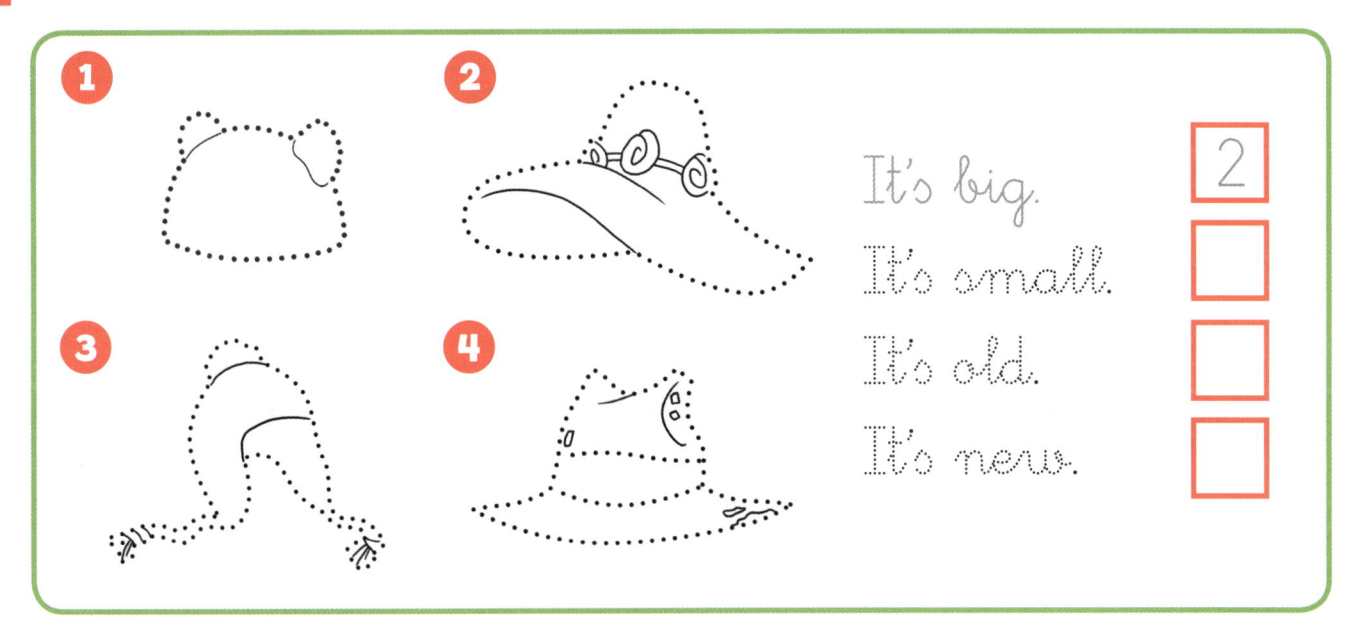

It's big. [2]
It's small. [ ]
It's old. [ ]
It's new. [ ]

Finished?
Write the words on this page with 3 letters.

1 Lesson 7 Literacy

Rooftops Book Club

1 Match and trace.

1. I'm Rosie.
2. I'm Ben.
3. I'm Grandpa.

2 Who is it? Look, read and trace.

1. Ben / Rosie
2. Grandpa / Ben
3. Rosie / Ben
4. Rosie / Grandpa
5. Grandpa / Ben
6. Ben / Rosie

Book Club Extra
Draw a book you like. Tell a friend.

Lesson 8 Communication

1 **Listen and tick ✔. Listen and chant.** 🔊 27

2 💬 **Communicate** Draw bingo cards. Play bingo with your friends.

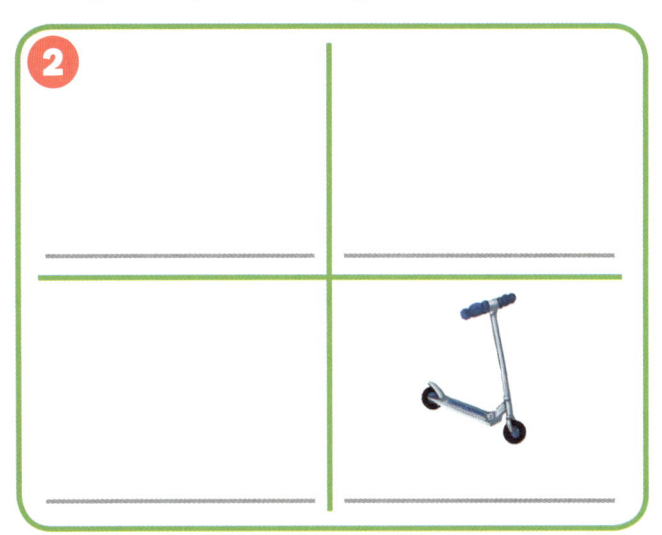

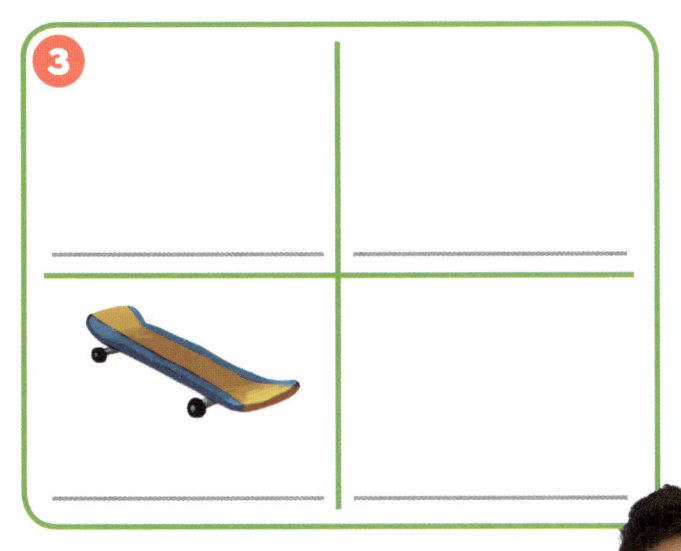

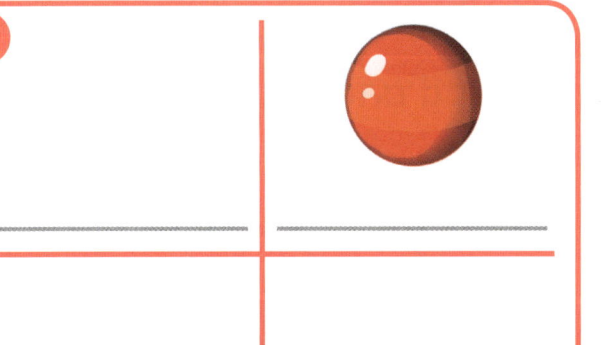

1. bike

2.

3.

4.

Bingo!

Pronunciation bike / book

Lesson 9 Round Up

1 Look, circle and write.

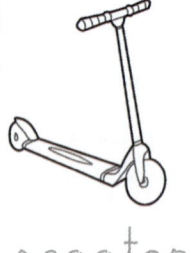

1. scooter

s	c	o	o	t	e	r
m	b	r	k	s	n	d
a	o	b	i	k	e	o
l	o	i	t	i	l	l
l	k	g	e	t	p	l
b	a	l	l	s	i	k

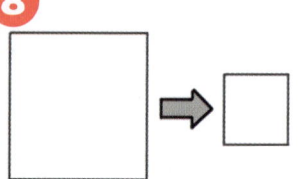

2 Read and circle. Trace, draw and colour.

I've got a bike / doll. It's new / old.

I've got a ball. It's small. It's red.

Finished?
Draw and write your favourite words in Unit 1.

14

Lesson 1 Vocabulary 2

2 By the river

1 Draw. Look and colour.   **2** Look and number.

dog ☐   mouse ☐   fish ☐   frog ☐
cat 1   rabbit ☐   bird ☐   horse ☐

Finished?
Draw the brown animals.

15

2 Lesson 2 Grammar

1 Look and number.

It's a ...

mouse ☐   fish ☐   rabbit ☐   cat ☐
horse ☐   dog ☐   frog [1]   bird ☐

2 Trace. Look and tick ✔.

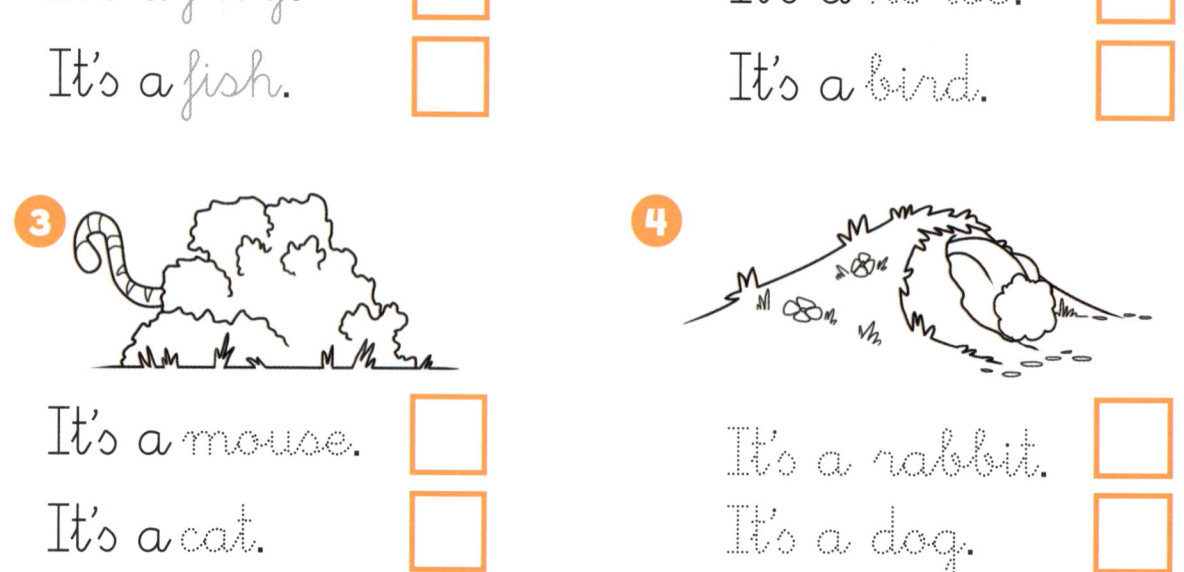

1.
It's a frog. ✔
It's a fish. ☐

2.
It's a horse. ☐
It's a bird. ☐

3.
It's a mouse. ☐
It's a cat. ☐

4.
It's a rabbit. ☐
It's a dog. ☐

Finished?
Write the words on this page with 4 and 5 letters.

Lesson 3 Culture **2**

1 Read. Tick ✓ or cross ✗.

It's a fish. ✓
It's purple. ☐

It's a frog. ☐
It's green. ☐

It's a horse. ☐
It's big. ☐
It's black. ☐

2 Be creative Draw an animal you can see where you live. Trace and write.

It's a _____.
It's _____.

17

Lesson 4 Everyday language and Values

1 Think Look and colour the children being kind to animals. Circle.

Our Values
Are you kind to animals?

(dog) / cat / fish

fish / dog / mouse

frog / rabbit / horse

bird / cat / horse

2 Communicate Trace. Ask your family. Write.

What's your favourite animal?

Name	Animal

The river story

Lesson 5 Story 2

1 🧠 **Think** Remember and match. **2** Trace and colour.

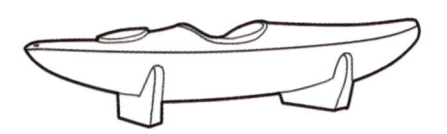

1.
2.
3.

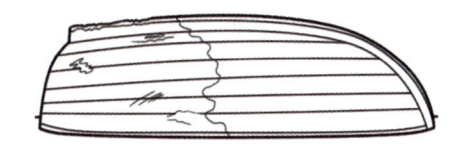

It's yellow.
It's green.
It's white.

3 💡 **Be creative** Look and colour Fergus. 🟡 🟢 ⚫ Write.

y_ _ _ _ _ _ nose

b<u>lack</u> body

_ _ _ _ _ _ legs

Finished?
Draw a boat. Colour and write *It's a ... It's ...*

2 Lesson 6 Vocabulary and Grammar

1 Look and tick ✓ what's missing. Draw.

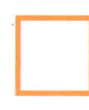

1. legs ✓ / nose ☐
2. body ☐ / nose ☐
3. legs ☐ / tail ☐
4. nose ☐ / tail ☐
5. body ☐ / legs ☐
6. body ☐ / nose ☐

2 Trace and write. Read and colour.

It's got ...
a brown tail,
a pink nose, orange legs
and a brown body.
It's a _____.

Finished? Write about Fergus.

Rooftops Book Club

Lesson 7 Literacy **2**

1 Find and circle.

Grandpa

arm

Rosie

Ben

kitchen

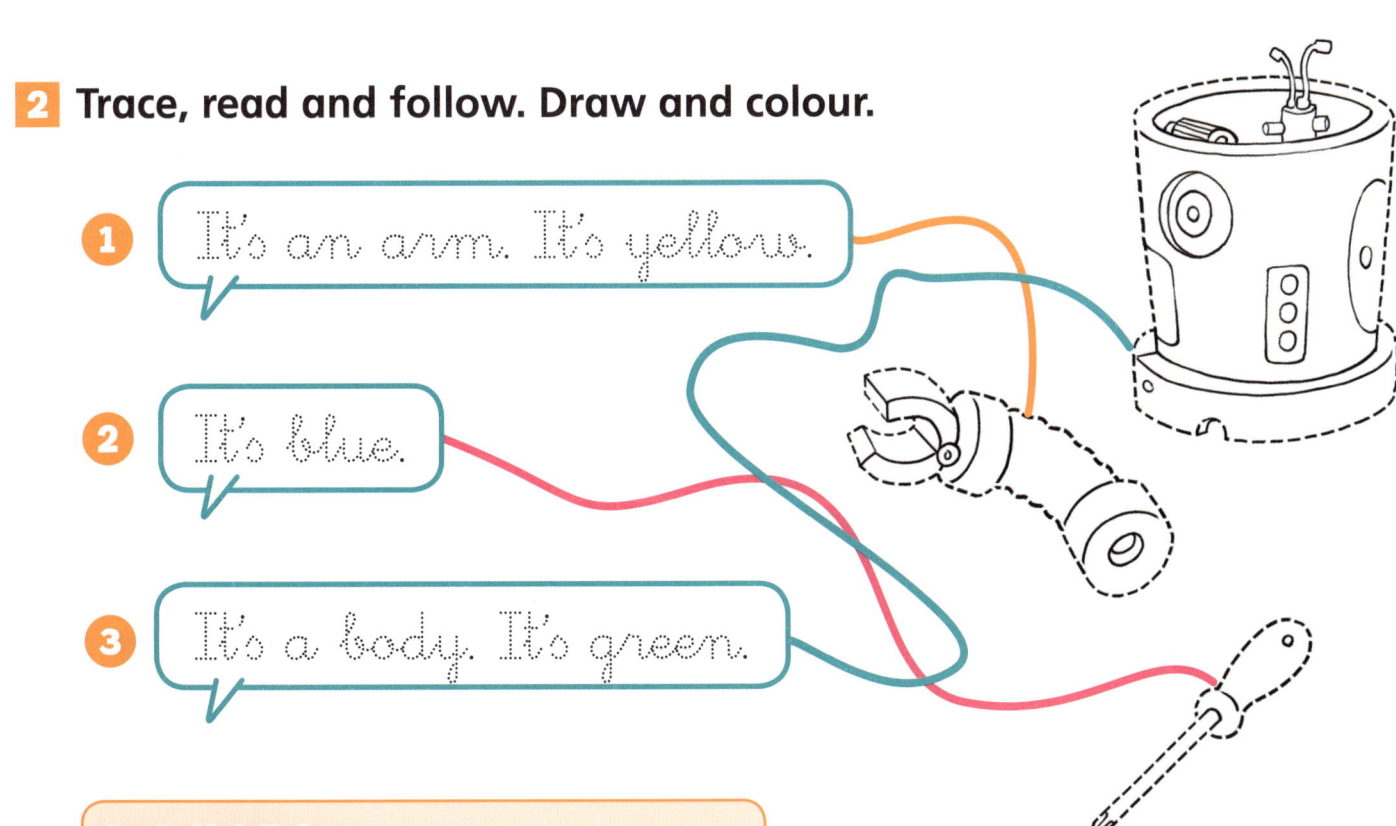

2 Trace, read and follow. Draw and colour.

1. It's an arm. It's yellow.

2. It's blue.

3. It's a body. It's green.

Book Club Extra
Draw a character you like. Tell a friend.

21

2 Lesson 8 Communication

1 Listen and tick ✓. Listen and chant. 🔊 47

2 💬 **Communicate** Choose, draw and colour an animal.
Describe, draw and colour with your friend.

cat   dog   mouse   bird

My animal

My friend's animal

It's got a red tail!

22 **Pronunciation** dog / doll

Lesson 9 Round Up 2

1 **Look and write.**

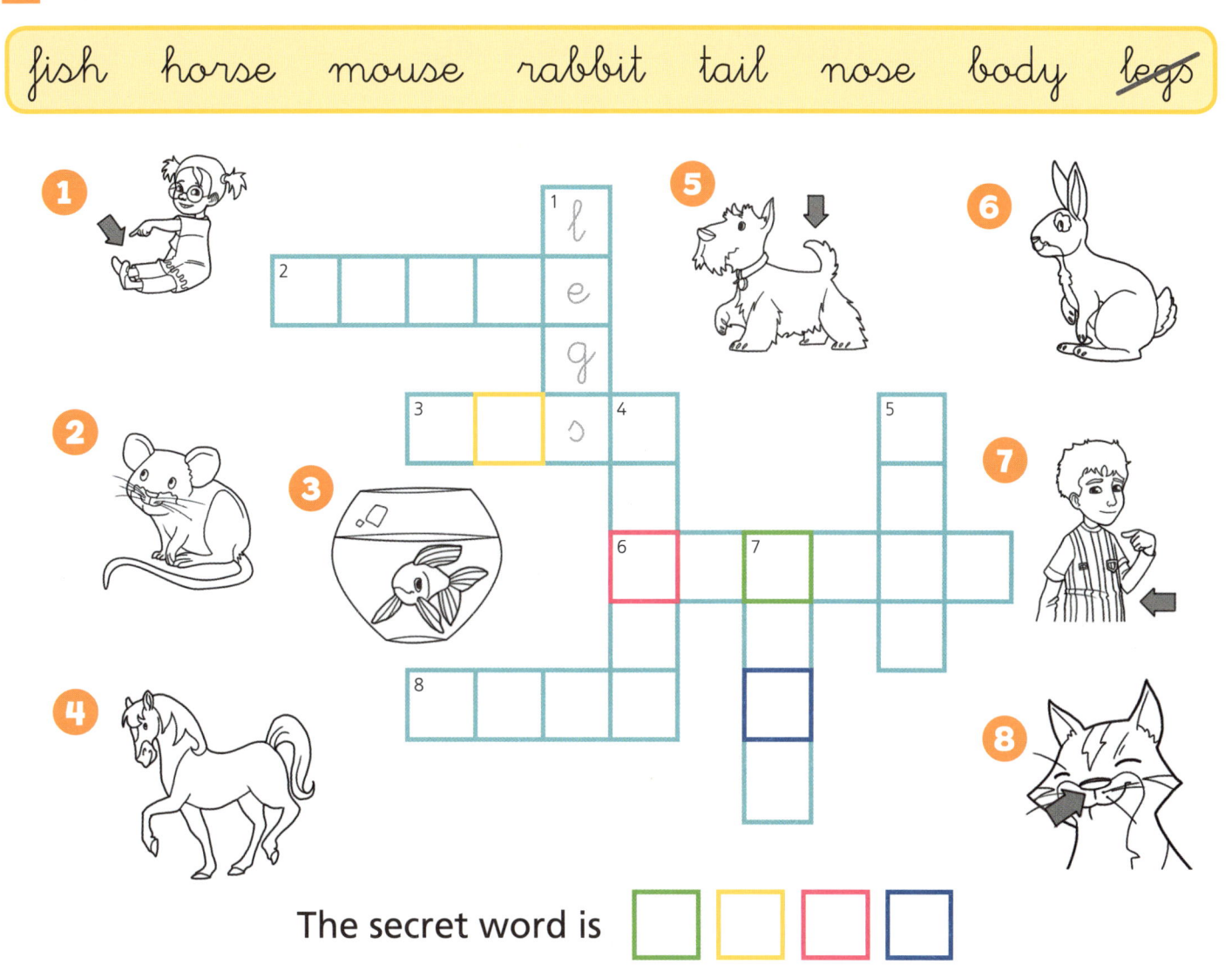

fish   horse   mouse   rabbit   tail   nose   body   ~~legs~~

1.
2.
3.
4.
5.
6.
7.
8.

The secret word is ☐ ☐ ☐ ☐

2 **Join the dots. Read and colour. Write.**

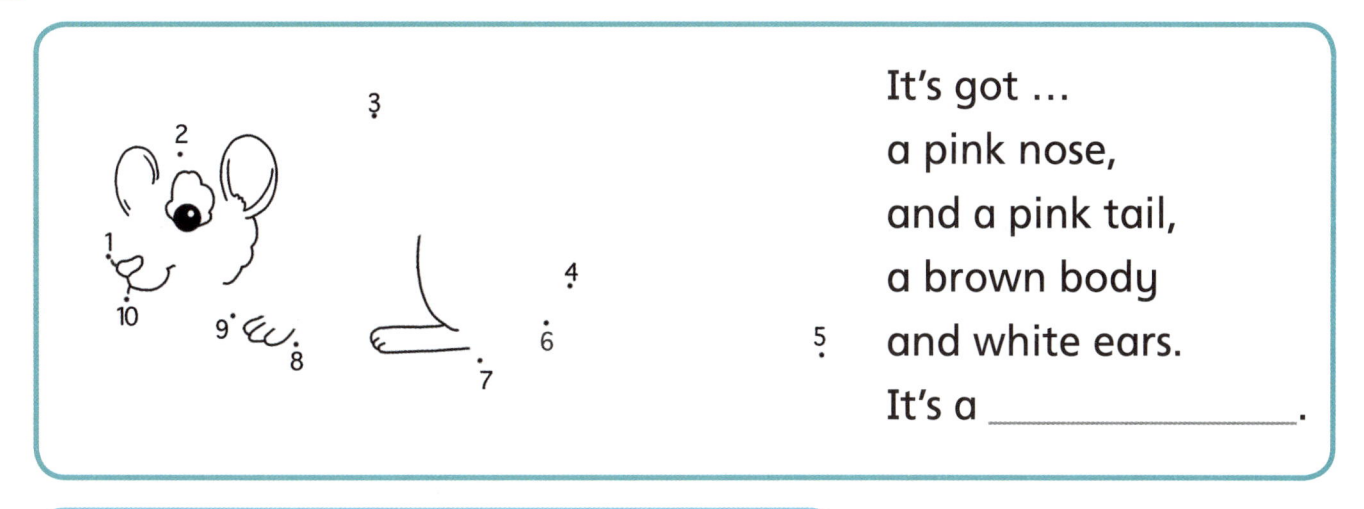

It's got …
a pink nose,
and a pink tail,
a brown body
and white ears.
It's a _____.

Finished?
Draw and write your favourite words in Unit 2.

23

Rooftops Review

1 💬 **Communicate** Trace. Find, point and say.

- a purple bike
- a black and white horse 
- a skipping rope 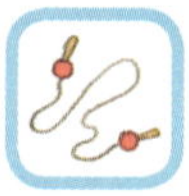
- a red fish
- Anna 
- a blue frog 
- a green 7 
- a big dog 
- a small kite 

Finished? Look and find!

Review 1

2 🗨 Think Sort and write the words.

red ~~doll~~ cat rabbit ball blue pink bike fish

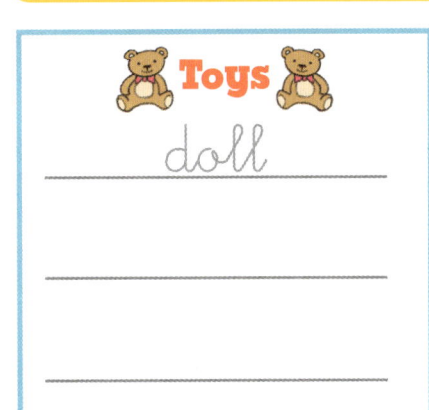

🧸 **Toys** 🧸	💥 **Colours** 💥	🐾 **Animals** 🐾
doll	

3 Follow, find and write.

~~skateboard~~ fish dog kite blue tail legs new

I've got a skateboard.
It's _____.

It's a _____.
It's got a red _____.

I've got a _____.
It's _____.

It's a _____.
It's got white _____.

Finished?
Look at Activity 2. Write one more toys, colours and animals word.

Lesson 1 Vocabulary

3 In the city

1 Look and number.   **2** Look and colour.

1 bus   2 train   3 car   4 taxi   5 lorry
6 motorbike   7 plane   8 helicopter

Finished?
Draw two kinds of transport. Write *It's a …*

Lesson 2 Grammar 3

1 **Colour and write.**

I can see a train.

~~train~~ bus plane car taxi
lorry helicopter motorbike

● train
●
●
●
●
●
●
●

2 **Read and draw. Trace and draw. Look and write.**

I can see a lorry.

I can see a car.

I can see a _____.

Finished?
Imagine! What can you see from the window? Draw and write *I can see a …*

27

3 Lesson 3 Culture

1 Listen and follow. Where are you? Tick ✓ and say. 🔊 57

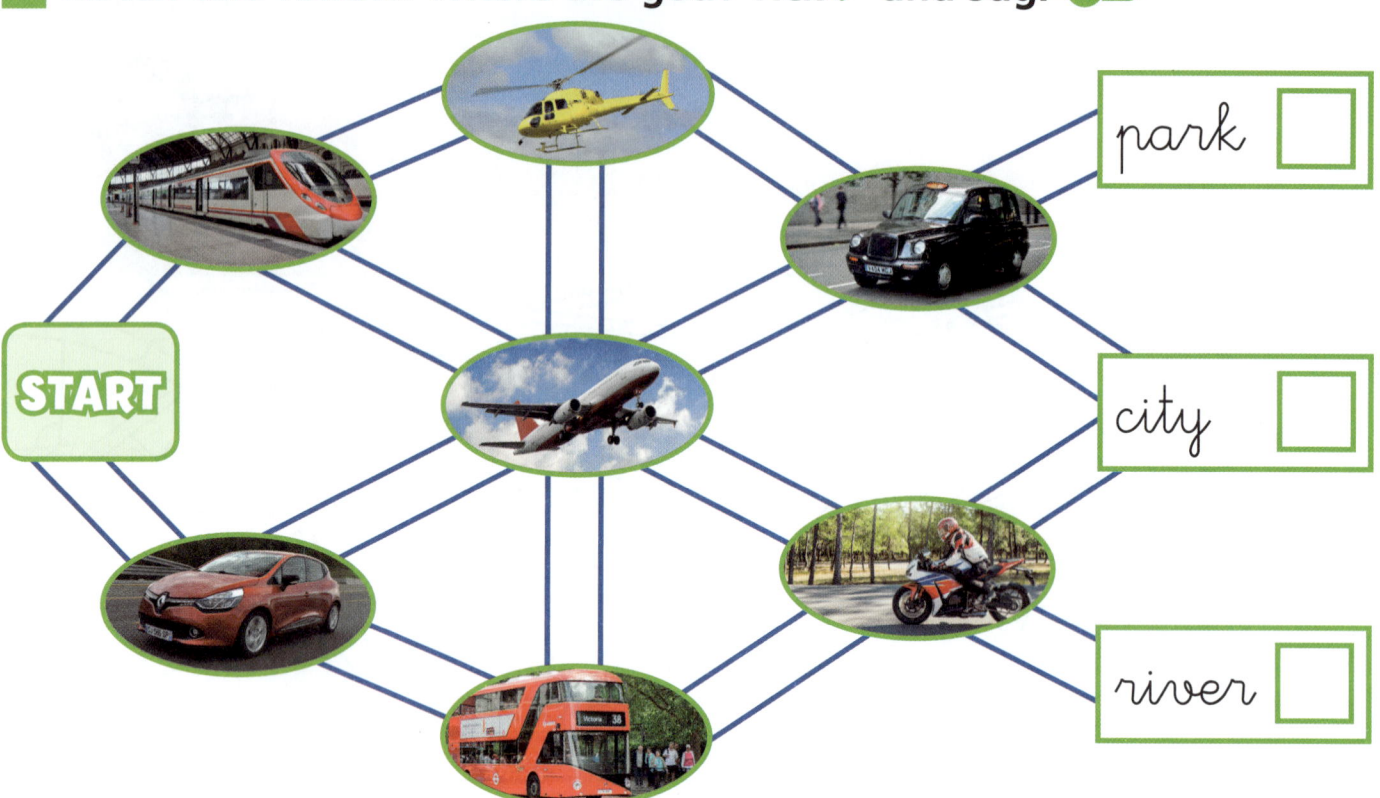

park ☐

city ☐

river ☐

2 💡 Be creative What can you see on your way to school? Draw and write.

I can see a _____.

Lesson 4 Everyday language and Values **3**

1 🗨 **Think** Who's thinking about others? Colour. Tick ✓ the words in the picture.

Our Values
Do you think about others?

car ☐
frog ☐
motorbike ☐
bike ☐
doll ☐
bag ☐

2 💬 **Communicate** Do you think about others? Trace. Act out at home.

Let's sit down!

Let's stand up!

3 Lesson 5 Story

The museum story

1 🗨 **Think** Number the pictures in order.

2 Read, look and tick ✓ or cross ✗.

[ ]   [ ]

[ ]   [1]

a bird [✓]   a tail [ ]   legs [ ]   a bike [ ]   a ball [ ]

3 💡 **Be creative** Draw and colour a mask.

Finished?
Draw something you can see in a museum. Write.

30

Lesson 6 Vocabulary and Grammar **3**

1 Follow and write.

walk   eat   ~~run~~   shout

1.
2. run
3.
4.

2 Trace. Make a sign for your class. Draw and write.

In the museum

1 Don't shout. ✗

2 Don't eat. ✗

In my class

Don't _____.

Finished?
Make a sign for your bedroom.

3 Lesson 7 Literacy

Rooftops Book Club

1 Look, draw and trace.

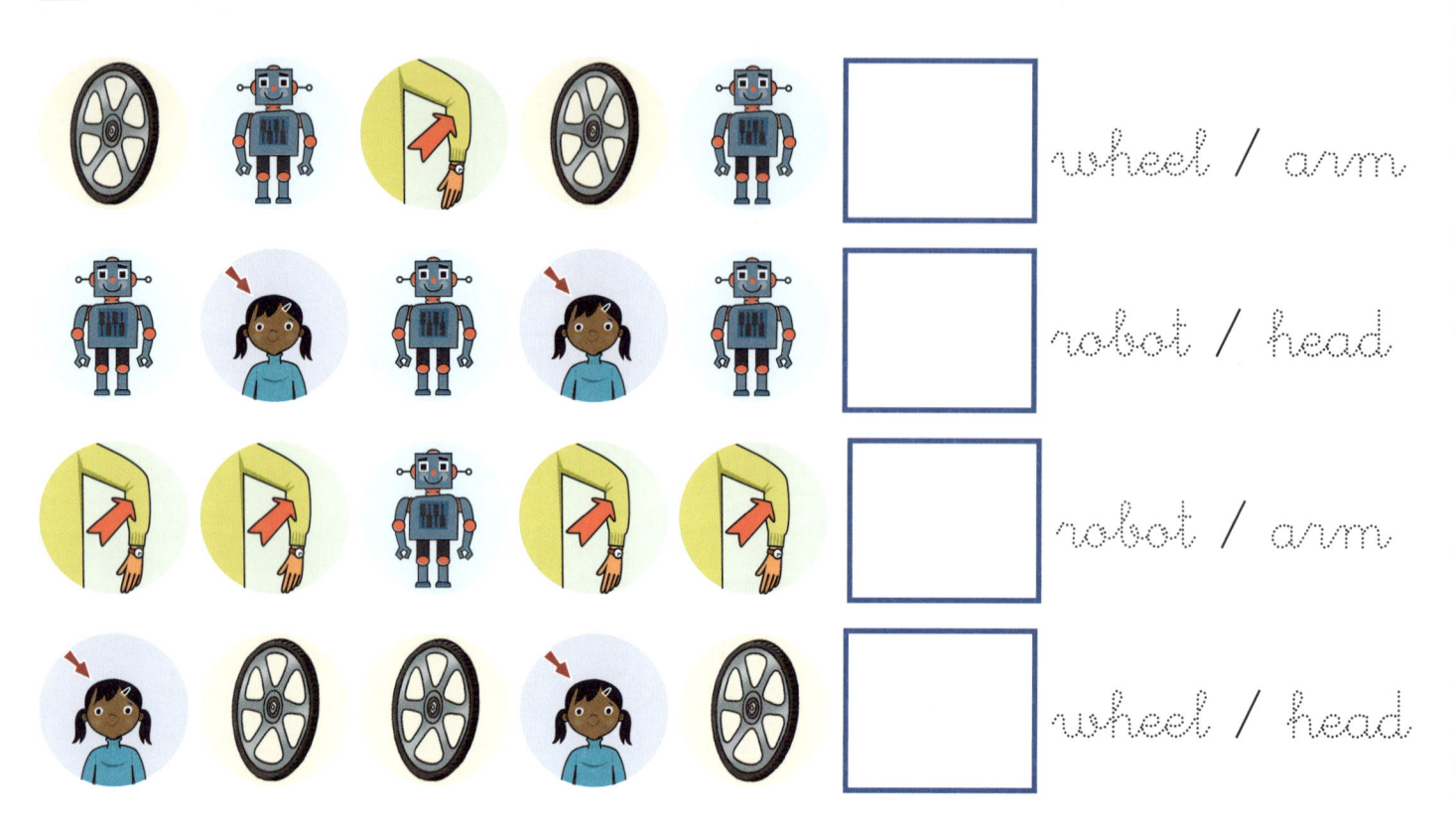

wheel / arm

robot / head

robot / arm

wheel / head

2 Read and tick ✔ or cross ✗.

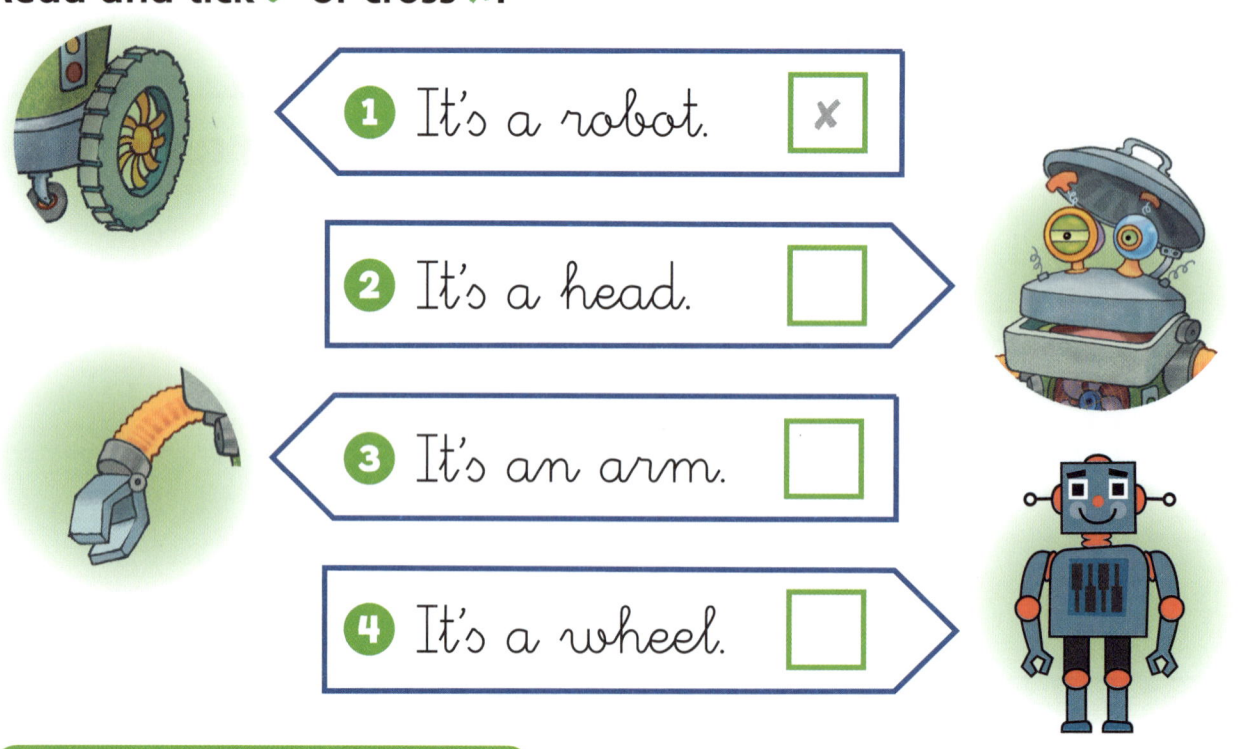

1. It's a robot. ✗
2. It's a head. ☐
3. It's an arm. ☐
4. It's a wheel. ☐

Book Club Extra
Correct the mistakes in Activity 2.

Lesson 8 Communication

1 Listen and tick ✓. Listen and chant. 🔊 68

2 💬 **Communicate** Play the transport game with your friends.

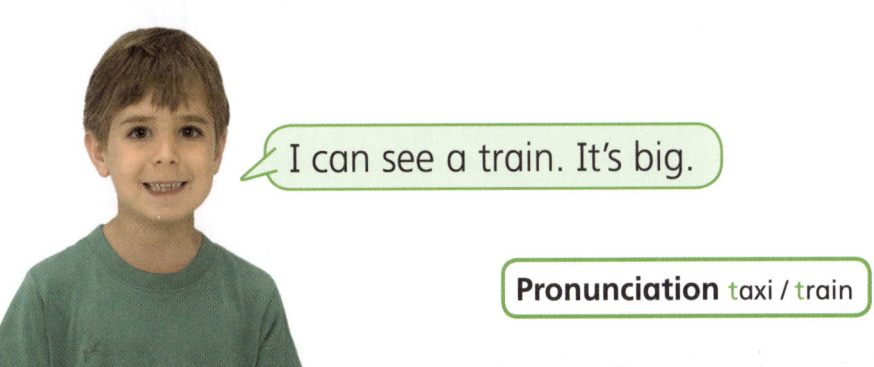

How to play
Take turns. Move your counter.
Talk about the transport.

Start

You need:

I can see a train. It's big.

Pronunciation taxi / train

Lesson 9 Round Up

1 Look, circle and write.

t	r	a	i	n	w	s
s	u	t	u	b	a	c
h	n	y	w	u	l	a
o	e	a	t	s	k	r
u	p	l	a	n	e	k
t	l	o	r	r	y	i

1. train
2.
3.
4.
5.
6.
7.
8.

2 Look and write.   I can see an   Don't   eat   airplane

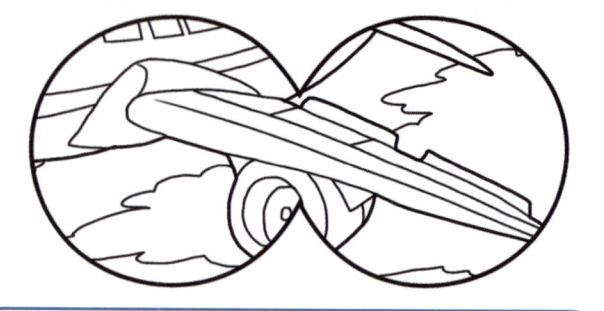

Museum Rules

Finished?
Draw and write your favourite words in Unit 3.

34

Lesson 1 Vocabulary

4 At the party

1 Look and number.   **2** Draw and colour the hats.

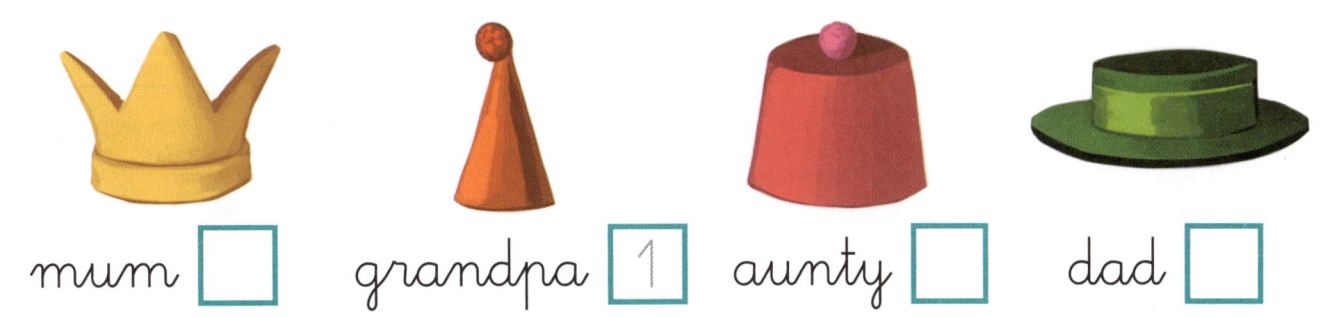

mum ☐   grandpa [1]   aunty ☐   dad ☐

brother ☐   grandma ☐   uncle ☐   sister ☐

Finished?
Who lives in your house? Write a list.

35

4 Lesson 2 Grammar

1 Look and write.

mum ~~dad~~ brother aunty grandpa grandma

1 This is my __dad__. 4 This is my _____.
2 This is my _____. 5 This is my _____.
3 This is my _____. 6 This is my _____.

2 Look, trace and write. uncle   sister

1 This is my _____. 2 _____.

Finished?
Draw a member of your family. Write *This is my …*

36

Lesson 3 Culture   4

1 Read. Tick ✓ or cross ✗.

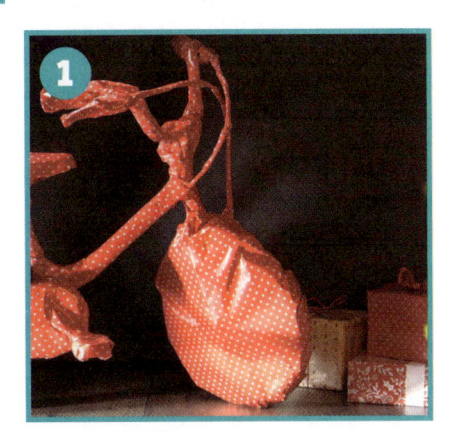

It's a book. ✗
It's a bike. ☐

I'm 7. ☐
I'm 5. ☐

This is my cake. ☐
This is my ball. ☐

2 💡 Be creative   Draw a birthday card for your friend. Write.

Happy birthday _____.
_____ years old.

4 Lesson 4 Everyday language and Values

1 🗨 Think   Colour the children playing nicely.
Look and tick ✓ the words in the pictures.

Our Values
Do you play nicely?

| helicopter | ✓ | Grandma | ☐ | cat | ☐ |
| horse | ☐ | doll | ☐ | skipping rope | ☐ |

2 💬 Communicate   Trace. Ask your family. Write.

How old are you?

Name	Age

Lesson 5 Story

The party story

1 💭 **Think** Number the pictures in order.   **2** Read and circle.

1. This is my grandpa / uncle.   2. This is my (grandma) / mum.

3. This is my aunty / uncle.   4. This is my brother / dad.

3 💡 **Be creative** Draw your party. Write.

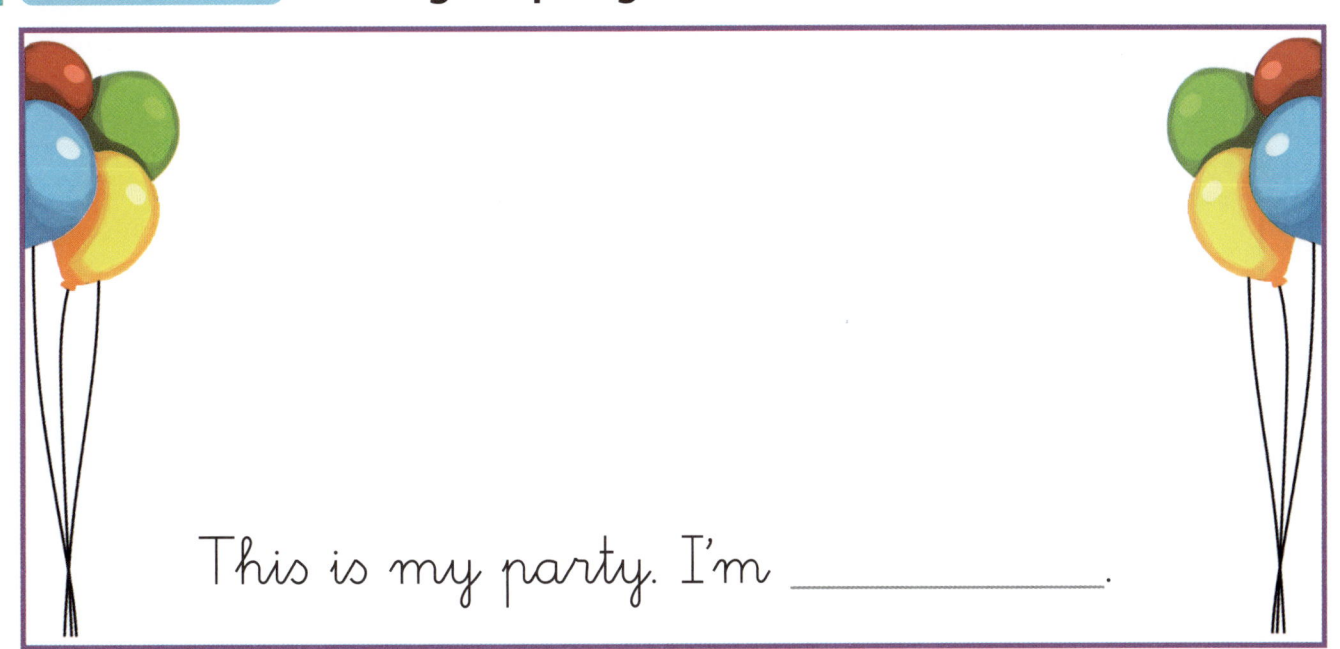

This is my party. I'm _____.

Finished?
Who's at your party? Write a list.

4 Lesson 6 Vocabulary and Grammar

1 Match and write.

~~skip~~   dance   sing   jump

1   2   3   4

_____   _____   skip   _____

2 Who is it? Write. Trace and circle. Write.

dad   Anna   mum

1. _____
He can jump.
She can jump.

2. _____
He can dance.
She can dance.

3. _____

Finished?
What can you do? Write the words.

Rooftops Book Club

Lesson 7 Literacy 4

1 Trace. Draw, colour and number.

1 arm   2 banana   3 head   4 wheel

2 Look at the picture. Read and tick ✓ or cross ✗.

1 I can see Clunk.   ✗

2 I can see a wheel.

3 I can see a banana.

4 Clunk can see a banana.

5 Rosie can see a banana.

Book Club Extra
Draw a robot.

41

4 Lesson 8 Communication

1 Listen and tick ✓. Listen and chant. 🔊 88

2 💬 Communicate   Play the family and friends game.

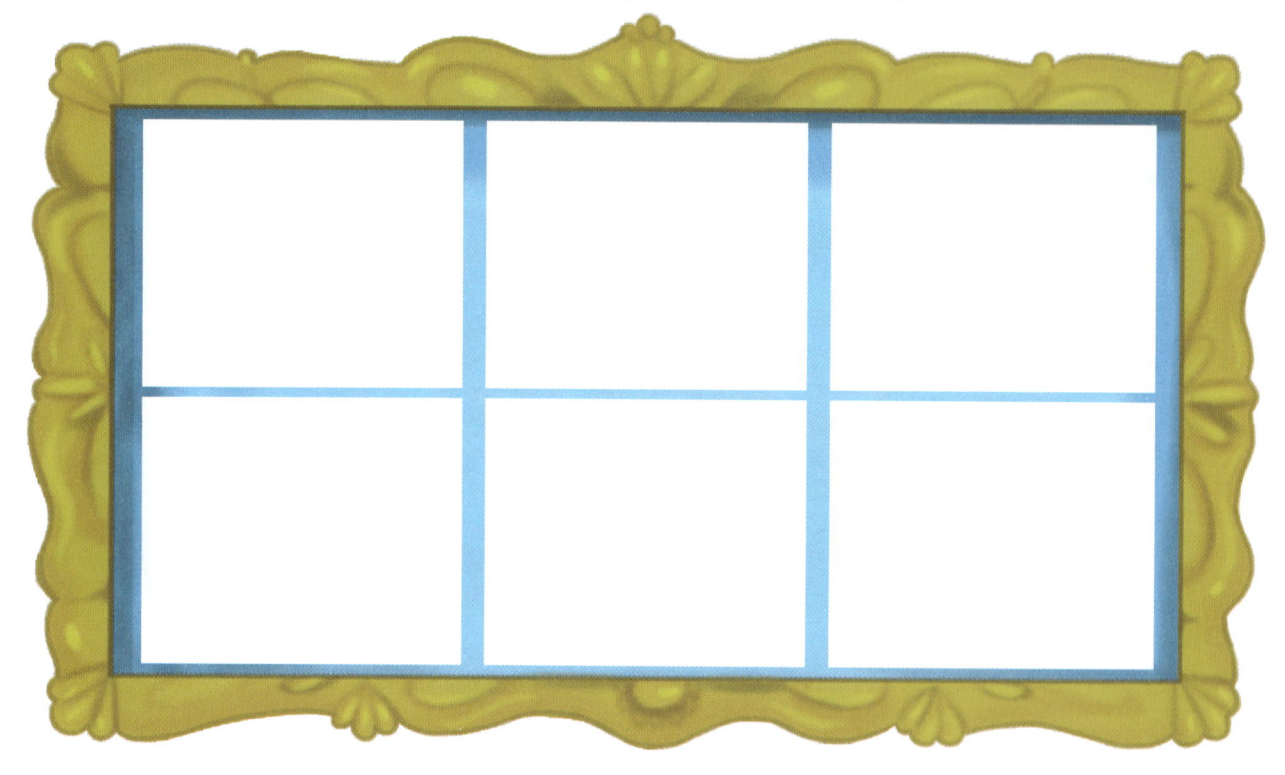

1 _____   4 _____

2 _____   5 _____

3 _____   6 _____

> This is my mum. She can dance.

You need:

How to play
Draw your family and friends.
Move your counter. Say and write.

42 **Pronunciation** mum / brother

Lesson 9 Round Up **4**

1 Look and write. Who's missing? Write.

mum   grandpa   aunty   dad
~~brother~~   uncle   sister

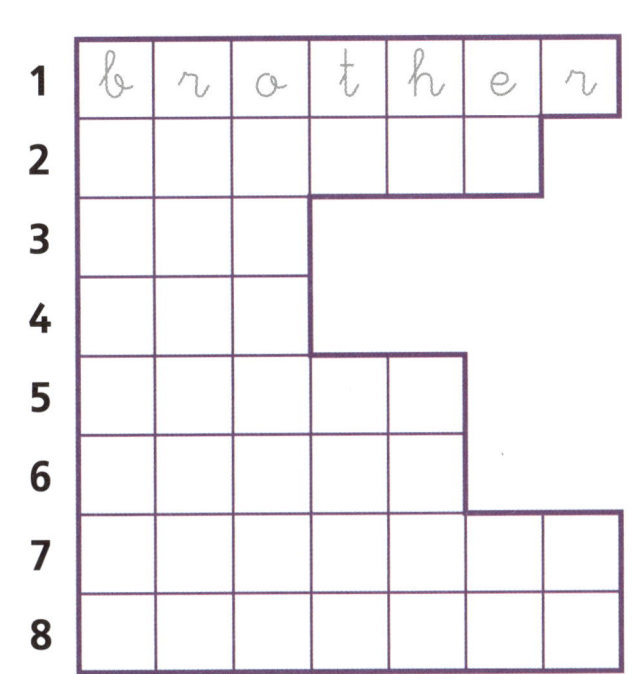

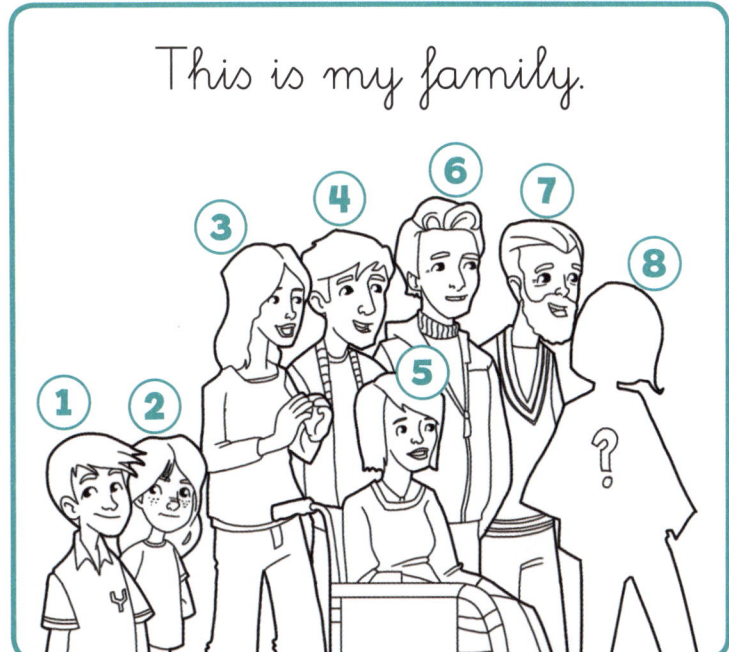

1 b r o t h e r
2
3
4
5
6
7
8

This is my family.

2 Look, circle and write.

1 This is my _____.

He can sing / jump / skip / dance.

2 This is _____.

She can _____.

Finished?
Draw and write your favourite words in Unit 4.

43

Rooftops Review

1 💬 **Communicate**   Trace. Find, point and say.

- 7 motorbikes
- 4 helicopters
- 1 bus
- 3 trains
- Mum
- Aunty
- sing
- dance
- dog
- 4 taxis
- shout
- grandma

2 Find and count. Say *I can see ...*

plane ☐   car ☐   dog ☐   bike ☐

Finished? Look and find! 🐦

44

Review 2

3 🌧 Think Sort and write the words.

bus ~~brother~~ skip dad lorry shout aunty plane run

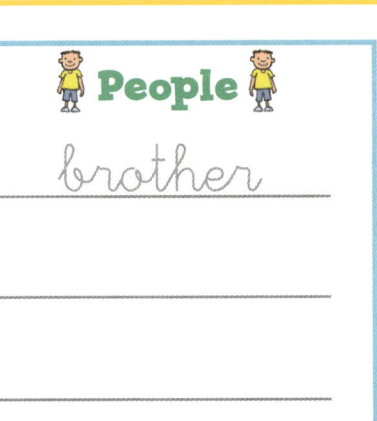

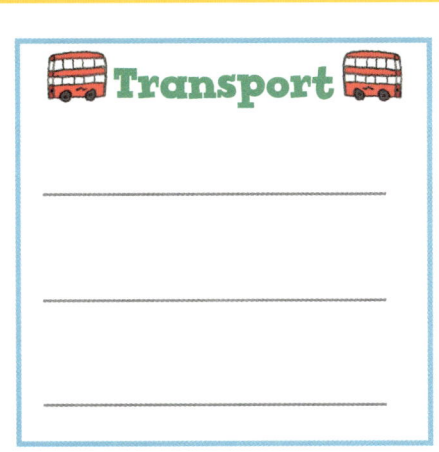

People

brother
_____
_____
_____

Transport

_____
_____
_____
_____

Actions

_____
_____
_____
_____

4 Follow. Look, trace and write.

He can   ~~Run~~   grandma   Don't walk
sing   I can see   This is my

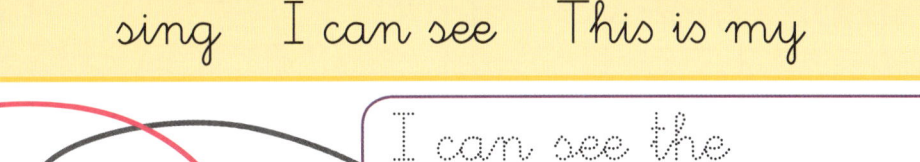

I can see the train. _____Run_____!

This is my _____.
She can _____.

_____ a can. _____.

_____ uncle.
_____ dance.

Finished?
Look at Activity 3. Write one more people, transport and actions word.

Lesson 1 Vocabulary

5 At the carnival

1 Read and colour.   **2** Circle and write.

cap   dress
jacket   shoes
skirt   T-shirt
sunglasses
trousers

1. h b a c c r a (c a p) s d — cap
2. y t t T-s h i r t h a k
3. l c a p t r o u s e r s
4. s k n s k i r t d r e j
5. c a d d r e s s j a t s
6. s h i s h o e s s u t
7. d s u n g l a s s e s p
8. t r o u j a c k e t s h

Finished?
What clothes can you see? Write *I can see …*

46

Lesson 2 Grammar 5

1 Look and write.

> cap   dress   ~~jacket~~   shoes   skirt
> sunglasses   trousers   T-shirt

1 I'm wearing a jacket.
2 I'm wearing _____.
3 I'm wearing _____.
4 I'm wearing _____.
5 _____
6 _____
7 _____
8 _____

2 Draw yourself at the carnival. Write.

I'm wearing
_____
_____
_____
_____.

Finished?
What are you wearing today? Draw and write.

5 Lesson 3 Culture

1 Listen and say *yes* or *no*. 🔊 98 Tick ✓ the clothes you can see.

cap	☐
dress	☐
jacket	☐
shoes	☐
skirt	☐
sunglasses	☐
trousers	☐
T-shirt	☐

2 💡 **Be creative** What can you do? Draw and write.

I can _____.

I'm wearing _____.

Lesson 4 Everyday language and Values **5**

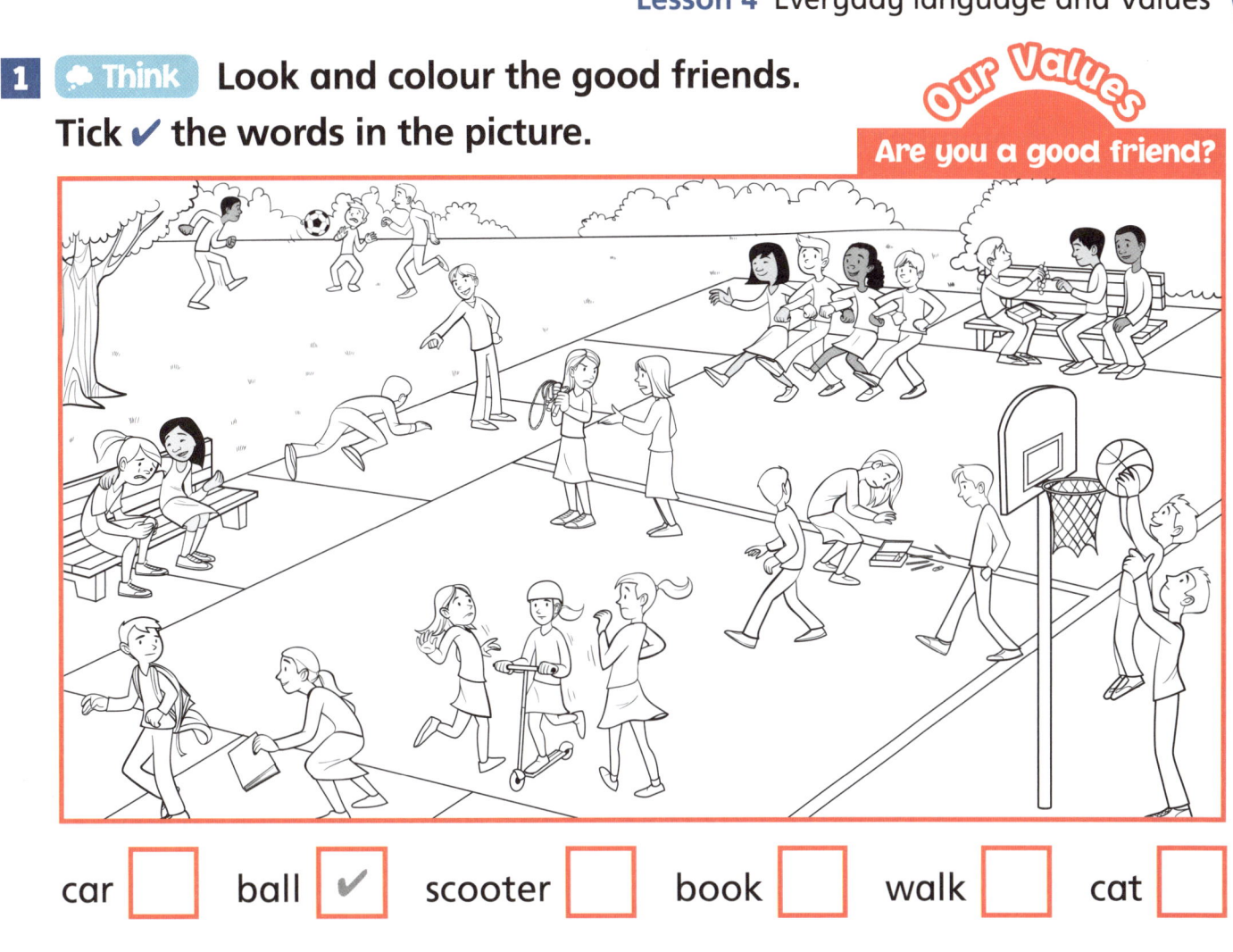

1 💭 Think Look and colour the good friends.
Tick ✔ the words in the picture.

Our Values
Are you a good friend?

car ☐   ball ✔   scooter ☐   book ☐   walk ☐   cat ☐

2 💬 Communicate Look, trace and write.
Play a mime game. Say and do.

trousers   cap

Put your _____ on.

Take your _____ off.

49

Lesson 5 Story

The carnival story

1 🗨 **Think** Number the pictures in order. **2** Read and match.

- Here's your T-shirt, your trousers and your mask.
- I'm a girl and I can dance and I can jump.
- I'm wearing my trousers and my T-shirt.

3 💡 **Be creative** Draw the clothes on the dancer. Read and tick ✓.

- T-shirt ☐
- dress ☐
- cap ☐
- trousers ☐
- jacket ☐
- shoes ☐
- sunglasses ☐
- skirt ☐

Finished?
What do you do at a carnival? Draw and write.

Lesson 6 Vocabulary and Grammar   5

1 Look and write.

hungry   sad   tired   thirsty   ~~happy~~

1 He's _happy_.   2 She's _____.   3 She's _____.
4 He's _____.   5 She's _____.

2 Draw and write.

1 He's _thirsty_.   2 _____

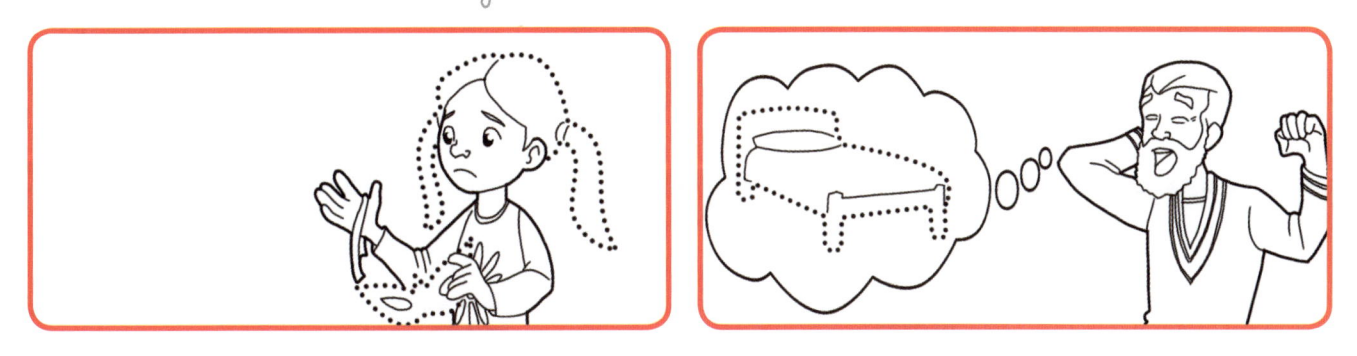

3 _____   4 _____

Finished?
How does your friend feel? Draw and write.

5 Lesson 7 Literacy

Rooftops Book Club

1 Follow and write.

Rosie   ball   book   banana   Yes   No

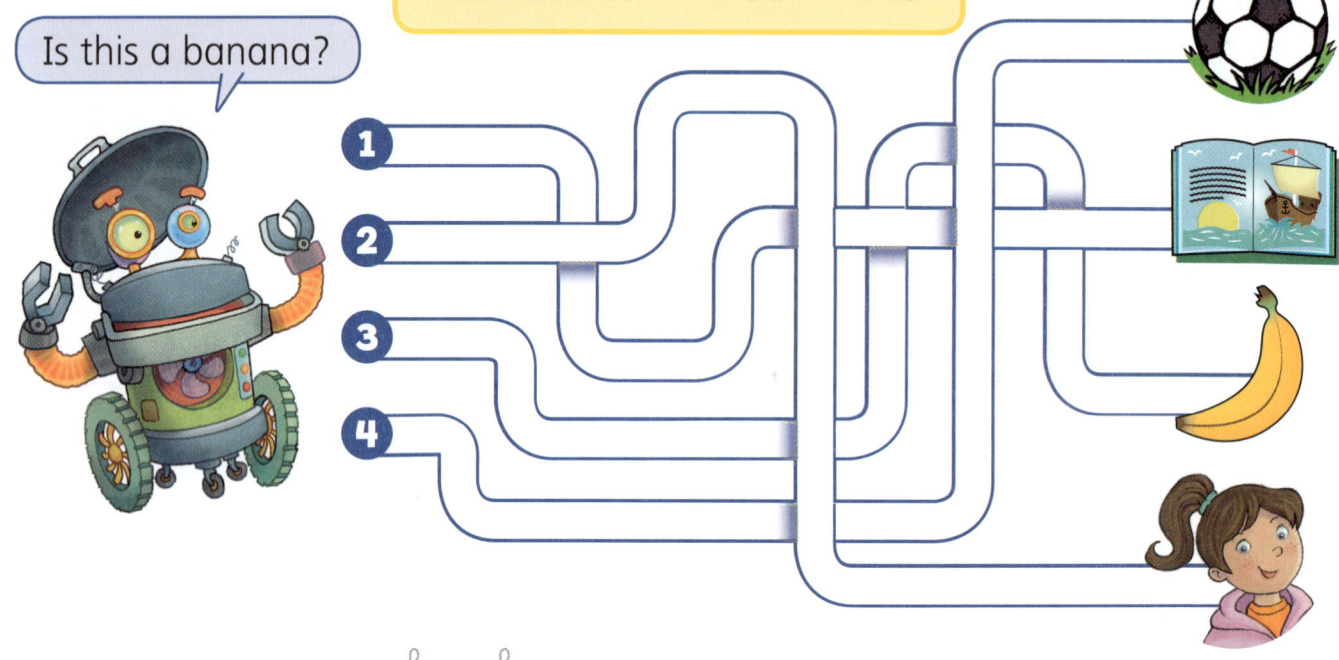

Is this a banana?

1   No, it's a ____book____ .   2   No, it's _____.

3   _____, it's a _____.   4   _____, it's a _____.

2 Read and tick ✓. Write.

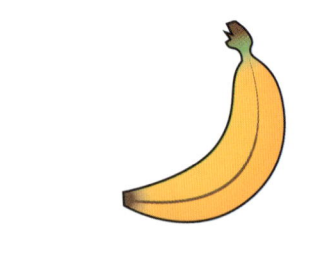

Is this a banana?

Yes, it's a banana. ☐

No, it's a ball. ☐

Is this a ball?

Yes, it's a ball. ☐

No, it's a wheel. ☐

Is this a book?

_____

_____.

Book Club Extra
Write and draw the words that begin with 'b'.

Lesson 8 Communication **5**

1 Listen and tick ✓. Listen and chant. 🔊 109

2 💬 Communicate Tick ✓ and draw your clothes. Describe and draw with your friend.

- cap
- dress
- jacket
- shoes
- skirt
- sunglasses
- trousers
- T-shirt

My friend's clothes

My clothes

I'm wearing a red cap.

A red cap … OK.

Pronunciation happy / hurray

5 Lesson 9 Round Up

1 Look and write. Circle and write.

cap   dress   jacket   shoes   skirt
~~sunglasses~~   trousers   T-shirt

1 _sunglasses_
2 _____
3 _____
4 _____
5 _____
6 _____
7 _____
8 _____

She's happy / hungry.

_____.

2 What are you wearing today? Draw and write.

I'm wearing _____
_____
_____
_____.

Finished?
Draw and write your favourite words in Unit 5.

Lesson 1 Vocabulary

6 At the picnic

1 Circle and draw.   **2** Write.

applescakessausageseggsolivestomatoes
strawberries(sandwiches)

1. sandwiches
2. ___
3. ___
4. ___
5. ___
6. ___
7. ___
8. ___

Finished?
Find the word with 12 letters. Draw and write.

6 Lesson 2 Grammar

1 Look, number and write.

apples   cakes   eggs   olives   sandwiches   sausages   ~~strawberries~~   tomatoes

I like *strawberries*.
I like _____.

I like _____.
I like _____.

_____.
_____.

_____.
_____.

Finished?
Choose 2 foods. Draw and write *I like …*

56

Lesson 3 Culture **6**

1 Read and number. **2** Look and circle your favourite farm.

1 This is my farm! Look! I've got apples and eggs!

2 This is my farm. I've got tomatoes and strawberries.

3 This is my farm. I've got sandwiches and cakes in the shop!

3 Be creative What grows near where you live?
Draw a farm and write.

I can see _____.

I like _____.

6 Lesson 4 Everyday language and Values

1 🍀 **Think**   Look and colour the healthy food.
Look and tick ✔ the words in the picture.

Our Values
Do you eat healthy food?

- olives ✔
- skirt ☐
- apples ☐
- cap ☐
- cakes ☐
- T-shirt ☐

2 💬 **Communicate**   Trace. Ask your family. Tick ✔. Circle the healthy food.

Do you like apples?

Yes, I do.

Name	🍓	🍏	🧁
___			
___			
___			

58

Lesson 5 Story **6**

The picnic story

1 💭 **Think** Number the pictures in order. **2** Read and match.

I like pears.

I've got olives.

I can see Anna.

3 💡 **Be creative** Draw yourself at the picnic. Write. Say.

I'm at the picnic. I like …

Finished?
Remember and write the picnic food in the story. Check and draw!

59

Lesson 6 Vocabulary and Grammar

1 Colour, count and write.

peaches   oranges   pears   cherries   grapes

8	peaches

2 Look and write. Draw for you and write.

1. I don't like _cherries_.
   I don't like _____.

2. _____
   _____

3. _____
   _____

4. ☺ _____
   ☹ _____

Finished?
Write food words in 2 lists ☺ and ☹.

Rooftops Book Club

Lesson 7 Literacy 6

1 Look and write.

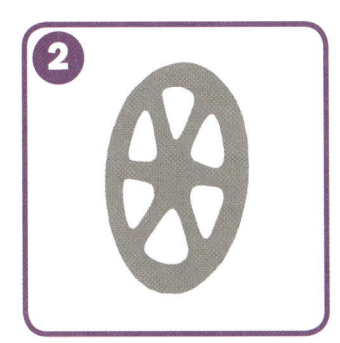

1	2	3
Grandpa	_____	_____

4	5	6
_____	_____	_____

> Ben
> Rosie
> ~~Grandpa~~
> wheel
> arm
> banana

2 Read and write. Draw Clunk and Rosie.

This is a _banana_. It's _____.
You can _____ it.

> ~~banana~~
> yellow
> I like
> eat

Thank you! _____ bananas.

Book Club Extra
What can you see on page 13 of your reader? Write a list! *I can see …*

6 Lesson 8 Communication

1 Listen and tick ✓. Listen and chant. 🔊 129

2 💬 Communicate Play the food game with your friends.

Go back ↓

Start ↑

You need:

How to play
Take turns. Move your counter.
Draw ☺ or ☹ and say.

I don't like oranges.

Pronunciation sandwiches / sausages

Lesson 9 Round Up **6**

1 Look, circle and write.   **2** Draw ☺ and ☹ for you.

t	o	m	a	t	o	e	s
o	r	a	n	g	e	s	a
n	p	e	a	r	s	m	u
c	h	e	r	r	i	e	s
a	q	p	f	e	s	g	a
k	v	o	t	k	a	g	g
e	c	s	a	n	r	s	e
s	p	e	a	c	h	e	s

1. sausages
2. _____
3. _____
4. _____
5. _____
6. _____
7. _____
8. _____

3 Draw 2 foods you like and 2 foods you don't like. Write.

I like _____.

I don't like _____.

Finished?
Draw and write your favourite words in Unit 6.

63

Rooftops Review

1 💬 **Communicate** Find and count. Write the number.

- cakes — 8
- yellow T-shirts
- thirsty boys
- hungry girls
- red skirts
- blue caps
- oranges
- sandwiches
- purple shoes
- tomatoes
- tired dads
- pink sunglasses

Finished?
Look and find Neena!

Review 3

2 🍃 Think   Sort and write the words.

~~grapes~~   cap   happy   hungry   dress   cherries
shoes   sad   eggs   tired   olives   trousers

🍎 **Food** 🍎

grapes
_____
_____
_____

👕 **Clothes** 👕

_____
_____
_____
_____

🙂 **Feelings** 🙂

_____
_____
_____
_____

3 Read, colour and draw. Draw and write about you.

I'm wearing a blue skirt and a yellow T-shirt.

I like sandwiches, cakes and cherries.

I'm happy!

_____
_____
_____

Finished?
Look at Activity 2. Write one more food, clothes and feelings word.

65

Happy Halloween

1 Look and colour. Tick ✓ your favourite costume.

bat   ghost   witch   monster   rat   pumpkin

2 Draw. Trace and tick ✓.

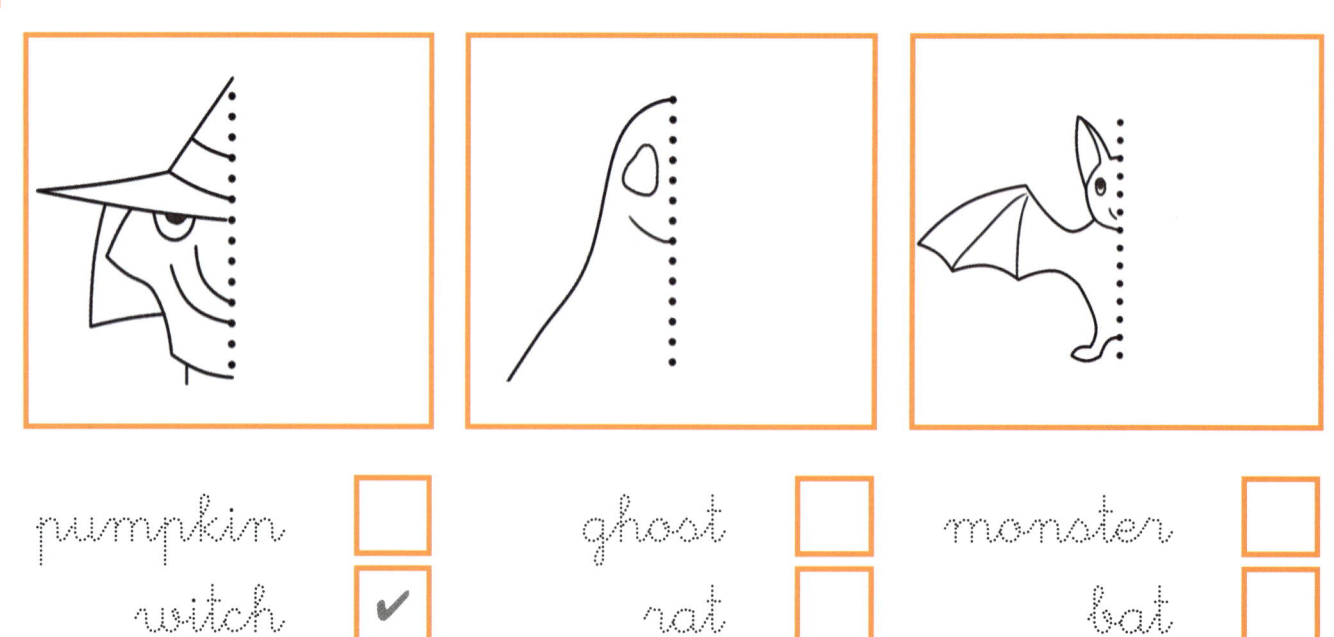

pumpkin ☐   ghost ☐   monster ☐
witch ✓   rat ☐   bat ☐

Merry Christmas

1 Colour the picture. Complete the key.

carrot = ●   present = ○   tree = ○
star = ○   stocking = ○   mince pie = ○

2 Look and write.

1. It's a _star_.
2. It's a _____.
3. It's a _____.
4. It's a _____.
5. It's a _____.
6. It's a _____.

Happy Easter

1 Look and colour. Count and write.   **2** 💬 Communicate Say.

Easter bunny   *basket*   *flowers*
hot cross buns   *Easter eggs*   *chicks*

I can see …

1	blue	*Easter bunny*	☐	brown	_____
☐	green	_____	☐	purple	_____
☐	pink	_____	☐	yellow	_____

6 At the farm shop

This book belongs to

Class _____

4 Here's a big strawberry.

5 Here's my aunty. Look, apples!

6 Make your mini-book.

7

My favourite food is _____.

2

Here's the farm. Look!
Carrots and tomatoes.

---

6 I'm at the picnic.

I can see strawberries.
Let's pick the strawberries. **3**

5 At dance club

This book belongs to
_____

Class
_____

4 This is my friend, Hayden. He can dance.

5 Look at me! I can dance.

5 Make your mini-book.

71

2 Now, I'm wearing grey trousers and a blue T-shirt. I'm wearing a yellow cap.

3 I'm wearing my school uniform. I'm wearing black trousers, a red jacket and a blue jumper.

6 This is the carnival.

7 _____

I'm wearing

4 At my party

This book belongs to _____

Class _____

This is my mum.
This is my friend Tyla.
Here's a tail. Let's play!

5

This is my grandma.
Thank you, Grandma.

4

4 Make your mini-book.

73

7 This is my cake. I'm _____.	**2** Hello! It's my birthday. This is my party.
6 This is my birthday party.	**3** This is my sister. Look, balloons! Blue, green, yellow and red!

3 In the city

This book belongs to

Class

I can see a black car.
It's a taxi.

4

I can see bikes.
Lots of bikes!

5

3 Make your mini-book.

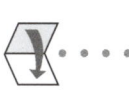

75

7	2
My favourite transport is _____.	Here's the city.
6 I'm in the city.	I can see a red bus. It's a big bus. 3

76

2 By the river

This book belongs to

Class _____

It's a dog.
It's big. It's black.

4

Look over there!
It's a horse. It's big.
It's brown and white.

5

---

2 Make your mini-book.

77

5

Here's the river.
Here's a barge.
It's green and brown.

7

My favourite animal.

6

I'm by the river.

3

Look! It's a bird. It's a goose.
It's big. It's white.

1 At the park

This book belongs to
_____

Class
_____

4 Look! A scooter!
It's pink and silver.

5 Here's my bag.
Here's my book.

1 Make your mini-book.

79

7 A toy for me.

2 Here's the park.

I've got a bike.
It's blue and black.
3

6 I'm in the park.

80